Beowulf Companion

*Includes Study Guide, Historical Context,
Biography, and Character Index*

BookCaps™ Study Guides

www.bookcaps.com

© 2013. All Rights Reserved.

Table of Contents

HISTORICAL CONTEXT 5

PLOT 8

THEMES 11

- HEROISM 11
- KINGS AND LINEAGE 12
- MONSTERS 13
- WEAPONS 14
- TREASURE 15
- PAGANISM 16
- CHRISTIANITY 17
- GENDER 18
- WATER 19
- LIGHT 20

CHARACTERS 21

- BEOWULF 21
- NARRATOR 22
- HROTHGAR 22
- HEALHTHEOW 23
- UNFERTH 23
- GRENDEL 24
- GRENDEL'S MOTHER 25
- HYGELAC 25
- HYGD 26
- THE DRAGON 27
- WIGLAF 28

CHAPTER SUMMARY 29

- PRELUDE 30
- I 31
- II 32
- III 34

IV	35
V	36
VI	37
VII	38
VIII	39
IX	40
X	41
XI	42
XII	44
XIII	45
XIV	46
XV	48
XVI	49
XVII	50
ABOUT BOOKCAPS	**51**
XVIII	52
XIX	53
XX	54
XXI	55
XXII	57
XXIII	59
XXIV	61
XXV	63
XXVI	65
XXVII	66
XXVIII	67
XXIX	69
XXX	71
XXXI	73
XXXII	75
XXXIII	76
XXXIV	78
XXXV	80
XXXVI	81
XXXVII	83
XXXVIII	85
XXXIX	86

XL 88
XLI 90

Historical Context

Beowulf is an epic poem detailing the heroic acts of the Anglo-Saxon warrior king, Beowulf. Originally, it was a legends told by the Geats in Scandinavia. Like most legends and myths, Beowulf's stories were passed down orally. The poems were most likely memorized and performed by traveling storytellers who made a living by going to different cities and towns to entertain the Geatish citizens. The legend of Beowulf is compared by scholars to the Iliad and Odyssey, the epic poems which shaped Greek literature.

While the legends were passed down through the generations through oral storytelling, the poem we have today is one written long after the legend of Beowulf was originally told. Historians believe that the poem originated at around 500 A.D. and was penned some two or three hundred years later, around 700 or 800 A.D. This disparity of time is clearly marked by the migration of the Anglo-Saxons to England, where the culture began to change.

In old Scandinavia, the societal structure was based on the middle ages warrior culture in which a strong king protected his people. Like many people in the feudal ages, the Geats had a pagan religion whose roots show through very clearly in Beowulf. Many historical figures who lived around the sixth century are also present in the poem, making it easy to guess when the stories originated.

The only known manuscript of the epic, however, was penned after the migration of the Geats to England. The most obvious clue to this conclusion is the fact that the anonymous narrator of Beowulf is Christian. It was only after the migration to England that the culture began to shift away from paganism and many people converted to Christianity. The Christian influences in the copy of Beowulf we read today were most likely not in the original stories, but rather added in order to merge the old culture with the new religion. The poem itself is written in old English, a very ancient form of Germanic English brought over from Scandinavia. While it is called old English, it is virtually unrecognizable by modern day English speakers.

Beowulf was not always a famous poem - in fact, it remained in relative obscurity and was almost burned in a fire during the 18th century. It was not until the 19th century that the epic was rediscovered, and new interest was brought to it. In the early 1900's, J.R.R. Tolkien, a British author and scholar, wrote a paper on Beowulf that caused the academic world to take the poem more seriously. Today, Beowulf is largely considered an original of English literature. It is taught in high schools and colleges all over the world, although in an easy to read translation of the original old English.

Plot

The warrior kings of Denmark began with Scyld, and after several generations his descendant, Hrothgar, came to rule. He was a just king and gathered builders from all over the world to build a great hall called Heorot. At Heorot, the people of Denmark came to drink and tell tales, and there was a time of peace. However, Grendel, a cursed descendant of Cain who lived in the swamp near Heorot became angry at their merrymaking. One night he entered the great hall and slaughtered thirty men. From then on, he terrorized Heorot and the surrounding countryside. He was so strong that no one could beat him, and tales began to spread of his strength and terror.

After over a decade, the tales spread to the land of Geat, where the great warrior hero Beowulf heard of them. Wanting to help Hrothgar and prove his worth, Beowulf set out with fourteen warriors to slay Grendel. Hrothgar is pleased but warns Beowulf that many men have tried to kill Grendel before and failed. Beowulf is so confident, however, that the Danes begin to believe in him.

That night Beowulf and his men camp in the great hall. Grendel approaches and is joyous to find warriors for him to kill. He eats one of Beowulf's men before the warrior, who was pretending to be asleep, grabbed Grendel's arm. A great fight ensues, and eventually Beowulf rips the shoulder and arm off. Realizing he is going to die, Grendel flees to the swamp, leaving his arm behind. Hrothgar is overjoyed at Beowulf's victory, and rewards him with treasure. They celebrate late into the night and fall asleep in the hall, unaware that the danger is not over.

Grendel's mother, also a strong and powerful demon, wants revenge. She enters the hall and kills one of Hrothgar's close friends, carrying his body back to her lair. Hrothgar once again asks Beowulf for help, and he agrees to go after her. They travel to the swamp and Beowulf begins to swim down to the depths. It takes him all day, but eventually he finds Grendel's mother and defeats her as well. He is given more treasure and sails back to Geatland victorious.

Eventually Beowulf becomes King when his kinsmen die, and reigns for fifty years. The time of peace ends when a thief accidentally steals a piece of treasure from a dragon underground. The dragon begins ravaging the countryside, and Beowulf realizes he must fight one more time. He chooses warriors to accompany him, and makes a great shield to defend against the dragon's fire. The dragon is about to overpower him when a young warrior named Wiglaf steps in and helps defeat the beast. Before the dragon dies, however, it bites Beowulf in the neck.

Realizing that he is about to die, Beowulf asks Wiglaf to bring him proof of the dragon's treasure. Wiglaf goes down and sees the immense pile of gold and jewels, bringing an armful back up to where Beowulf is resting. After seeing the treasure, Beowulf dies in peace. After Beowulf dies, Wiglaf is ashamed at the other warriors for being too cowardly to help during the battle.

Messages are sent throughout Geatland, and the people worry that without Beowulf to protect them war is imminent. The hero's body is burned at a funeral pyre and then buried, along with vast amounts of treasure and armor, in a barrow. His people viewed him as one of the greatest kings, and made sure that his name would never be forgotten.

Themes

Heroism

At its root, Beowulf is a story about a hero. But not just that, Beowulf embodies many heroic ideals commonly found in the middle ages, centering on bravery, strength, and honor. Beowulf is inhuman in his strength, but he is wise and just as well. He does not get in unnecessary fights or purposefully pick on those less strong than he is; instead he uses his strength to defend those weaker than himself. Heroes such as Beowulf are very common in legends and myths, and they adhere to a strict code of honor. In this sense, Beowulf is a very typical hero of ancient culture.

Kings and Lineage

In the feudal era, kings were of utmost importance to society. They won their positions by being the strongest warrior in the land. An ideal king was strong and would be able to protect their people from other violent influences and wars. In Beowulf, the first great warrior king of Denmark was Scyld, and from him many generations of kings were born. Lineage was very important to everybody, and many knew others not only by their name but by their father's name as well. Beowulf's father, for instance, although already deceased by the time the poem begins, is repeatedly brought up in conversation and his good reputation is added to Beowulf's.

Monsters

In Beowulf's world, monsters threatening the peace of humanity abound. Monsters serve as a way for heroes to show their strength and gain a reputation by slaying as many strong monsters as possible. The poem is divided up into three major fights in which Beowulf faces Grendel, Grendel's mother, and finally a terrifying dragon. According to the narrator, Grendel and his mother are both descendants of Cain along with all the monsters in the rest of the world. In this perspective, these fictional monsters represent the twisted and warped parts humanity that the heroes must fight against.

Weapons

What would a hero be without a legendary weapon? In Beowulf, special attention is given to impressive weapons, especially swords. During his second fight with Grendel's mother, another warrior named Unferth lends Beowulf his family sword, passed down through the generations. Later, Beowulf finds a legendary sword used by giants that was said never to have lost a battle. The weapons, it seems, have just as much to their reputation as the heroes who wield them. Although Beowulf proves that he is a hero without the use of a weapon when he faces Grendel completely unarmed in order to gain more glory.

Treasure

One of the benefits of going around slaying monsters was acquiring rare and ancient treasures. Either taken from the monster's lair or given as payment, treasure was a very important aspect of Beowulf's story. Beowulf is rewarded with great treasures for defeating both Grendel and his mother. However, he does not keep the treasure for himself but gives it freely to his kinsman Hygelac. Valuable treasures were passed down in families and served as important heirlooms in society. After Beowulf slew the dragon, he was thankful that he would leave so much treasure for his people as his legacy. In many respects, the value of treasure was not in the gold and jewels but rather in reputation and history.

Paganism

Although the narrator of Beowulf is Christian, there is still a definite influence of paganism throughout the stories in the poem. When Hrothgar and his people become terrorized by Grendel, the wise men convene and send offering to the gods in order to appease them. Even Grendel and the other monsters have roots in ancient pagan culture, although a Christian spin is put on them by explaining them as the descendants of Cain. The culture of heroes and slaying monsters is definitely from the old world of Scandinavia.

Christianity

Although the original myths did not include Christian influences, the anonymous writer who penned the poem added Christianity throughout the legends. The characters themselves rarely mention The Lord or refer to the Christian religion; the narrator, however, frequently interjects with observations about the actions and motivations of the characters, painting them in a good or bad light based on how much they coincide with Christian morals and values. There are many points where the Christian narrator seems to struggle with equating the old stories with the new way of looking at the world.

Gender

The middle ages were a time of very strict gender roles. Men took the role of powerful protector, and women gentle housekeepers. The poem touches on the issue of gender briefly by comparing Hygelac's queen, Hygd, with an ancient queen who was arrogant and violent. The narrator makes it clear that the ideal woman is gentle, beautiful and wise. The most interesting case in Beowulf is Grendel's mother, a swamp demon who has lost all semblance of femininity and is considered a warped being. She takes on a very active, masculine role in avenging her son and is eventually punished for it by Beowulf.

Water

In Beowulf, water is the symbol of ancient and unknown things. Both Grendel and his mother came from the swamp, which is reminiscent of the primordial waters in ancient creation myths. Hrothgar warns Beowulf that the bottom of the swamp waters has never been explored. Beowulf, being the hero, makes it down to the bottom while fighting off numerous sea monsters. Under water, he does not have his full strength and it is almost as if the water weakens him. Later, when the dragon dies, the warriors push its body off a cliff and into the water below.

Light

Just as water signifies ancient places and darkness, light continually acts throughout the poem as a signifier of God and heroism. When Beowulf kills Grendel's mother, a light shines out through the dark waters allowing Beowulf to find Grendel's body. The narrator makes many references to God being associated with light, and monsters with darkness. Even the dragon dwells in a vast underground cave and only after it is defeated can the warriors explore the cavern using torches and golden banners to light their way.

Characters

Beowulf

The protagonist and namesake of the poem, Beowulf is a man of great power who seeks glory by slaying monsters and helping others. He is from Geatland, and comes from a noble family. He seeks honor and glory at the risk of his own life, as shown when he decided to face Grendel without weapons or armor so that it would be an even match. Eventually Beowulf became king of the Geats, and was loved by all. He gave his life slaying the dragon that was terrorizing his country and was revered after his death.

Narrator

While the narrator of Beowulf is not named nor does he ever appear, his writing sets the stage for all the action to take place, and his comments frame how the reader is supposed to think about the events and the characters. Originally, the legends of Beowulf had no Christian influences, but since the narrator is writing the poem from a Christian standpoint he adds to the poem to create a bridge between the old and new cultures of the Anglo-Saxon people.

Hrothgar

The elderly warrior king of Denmark, Hrothgar is descended from a long line of warrior kings. He built the great mead hall named Heorot as a symbol of his peaceful and prosperous reign. Even in his old age, Hrothgar was well respected by his people and he was crushed when Grendel began terrorizing not only Heorot by the rest of the country as well. When Beowulf successfully defeats Grendel and his mother, Hrothgar shows all the necessary courtesy and treats Beowulf as his own son.

Healhtheow

Hrothgar's queen, Healhtheow joins him at all the important feasts. She wears a large amount of gold jewelry, and, fittingly, awarded Beowulf with several of the more valuable treasures for killing the monsters that threatened Denmark. In Heorot, Healhtheow was the picture of the perfect hostess and acted kindly towards Beowulf and his warriors.

Unferth

A Dane warrior who is envious of Beowulf's fame throughout the country. The night before Beowulf faces Grendel, Unferth tries to mock him by saying that he is not as strong as he needs to be to defeat Grendel and that he lost a swimming match to his friend Breca when they were young. Beowulf counters these insults with his version of events in which he slew hundreds of sea monsters during the swim and still beat Breca, winning the confidence of the Danes. Later, Unferth apologizes and even lends Beowulf his family sword in recompense.

Grendel

Grendel is an evil descendant of Cain who lives in the swamp near the great hall of Heorot. He heard the Danes' merrymaking and became angry, slaughtering thirty men the first night and continuing his rampage for over a decade. Grendel has no reason to be evil other than he was born of a traitor and a murderer. Many scholars believe that he symbolizes the original evil in mankind because he seems to be part human and part monster. During his fight with Beowulf, Grendel has his shoulder and arm torn off by Beowulf and flees to the swamp to die.

Grendel's Mother

Like Grendel, Grendel's mother is also an evil descendant of Cain. She comes out of the swamp after her son is killed seeking revenge on those who hurt him. While she is just as vicious as her son, she is not as strong and is forced to flee Heorot after only killing one person. Beowulf chases her underwater, and after a battle in which he is almost killed himself, slays her with a giant's sword. When she is dead, a light appears and all the sea monsters are gone from the waters. Like Grendel, she symbolizes the abstract evil present in man.

Hygelac

The king of Geatland and one of Beowulf's few kinsmen, Hygelac is an honorable and well-loved king in the poem. Although he only appears for one scene, he and Beowulf appear to be very close. He is greatly relieved to see Beowulf safe after defeating Grendel. Beowulf, being loyal to both kinsman and king, gives all the treasure he earned from his adventures to Hygelac, who in turn rewards Beowulf with lands and riches.

Hygd

Hygd is Hygelac queen, hailed for her gentleness and beauty. She is contrasted in the poem to an ancient queen who frequently had people killed just for looking at her in a way she didn't like. Hygd is nothing like this, and is praised for embodying the gentle feminine standards of the Anglo-Saxon culture.

The Dragon

The third and final monster that Beowulf faces, the dragon is an ancient creature who was cursed to horde treasure found in graves. He finds a vast cavern full of treasure amassed by a man who was the last of his clan. The dragon guarded the cave for three hundred years until a servant accidentally found the cave and ran out with a golden goblet. The dragon ravaged the countryside, eventually burning down Beowulf's throne and forcing him to fight. Unlike Grendel and his mother, the dragon does not have any sort of humanity about it, and is killed unceremoniously. For killing the dragon, Beowulf is compared to the greatest hero of all time, who also killed a dragon.

Wiglaf

Wiglaf is a young Geatish warrior who helps Beowulf defeat the dragon when all the others run towards the woods in fear of the beast. Wiglaf has a strong sense of honor and courage and reprimands the other warriors, calling them cowards for running away. He is with Beowulf at the very end, and before the hero dies he gives the young warrior his armor. At the end of the poem, Wiglaf seems like the most likely successor of Beowulf since he has no heirs.

Chapter Summary

Prelude

Beowulf opens hailing the great warrior kings of Danes. The first of these kings was named Scyld the Scefing. Although he was abandoned by his parents, he was very strong and soon rose to power. When he became king, his subjects showered him with gifts and honor. Soon, Scyld had an heir, a boy named Beow. He became famous and earned the loyalty of all his father's clansmen.

Sadly, Scyld died in battle before he reached old age, and requested to be returned to the ocean. His people loaded a ship with all sorts of treasures, armor and weapons and placed him on it. They hoisted a gold banner before sending the ship out to the ocean, as Scyld had wanted. The people grieved deeply at their king's passing.

I

Beow, having already become well-known and well-loved, became king after his father passed away. Eventually, his heir Halfdane succeeded him. Halfdane had a reputation for being a wise man, and was blessed with four children. He had three sons, Heorogar, Hrothgar and Halga, as well as one daughter who became the Queen of Swedes.

Hrothgar was a glorified warrior, and soon became famous throughout the land. He decided to build a great hall from which to rule from, and brought builders from all over the world to construct it. When it was completed, Hrothgar named the hall Heorot. Here Hrothgar ruled, as well as distributed gifts and drank with his men.

The clansmen lived in a time of peace, and enjoyed many years of drinking and merry making. However, that peace ended when Grendel, a descendant of Cain, came out of the swamp. Grendel was banished to exile by the creator, and spent his life among the other evil descendants of Cain. These included bad spirits, elves and giants. Despite the fact that they would never win, these evil forces continually battled against the Creator.

II

One night Grendel came out of the swamp and listened to the revelers singing and partying. After they fell asleep, he went inside the great hall and slaughtered thirty of the men before going back to his lair. At dawn, the men awoke and realized that there had been a massacre in the night. The people began mourning, and the leader of the Danes trailed Grendel back to his lair. They did not find him, however, and the next night Grendel struck again.

Eventually the great hall stood empty. For twelve years Grendel terrorized the country, bringing sorrow wherever he went. The people began spreading tales about how Grendel's hatred for Hrothgar and his people. Grendel refused to make peace with the men, and could not be bought with gold. He preyed on the young and old alike, and everyone was terrified of him.

Hrothgar was grief-stricken because he could not hold Heorot. He brought together the nobles of the land and any wise men he could find to see if they had any ideas. However, nothing could be done and they made offerings to the pagan gods because they did not have any ideas. The narrator points out that they did not know they could ask for help from The Lord.

III

Eventually, the tales of Grendel spread to surrounding countries. Beowulf, a relative of Hygelac, was the greatest warrior of the Geats. When he heard of Grendel, he decided to help Hrothgar. Although he was loved by his people, they let him leave and blessed him. Beowulf chose fourteen of the boldest men in the kingdom and prepared for the journey. The fourteen warriors, fully armed with mail and weapons, boarded a ship to cross the sea. They sailed to Hrothgar's land, and eventually landed safely. They climbed ashore and prayed to the gods, thanking them for safe passage.

A Scylding clansman, watching from a cliff, saw the warriors come ashore. He saw their glittering armor and weapons, and wondered what kind of men they were. Immediately, he got on his horse and rode down to find out. When he got closer, he pointed his spear at them and began asking questions. Although he noticed that one of the warriors looked like a great hero, he was still suspicious because they might be spies. He threatens them to speak quickly and tell him why they have come ashore.

IV

The leader of the warriors begins to speak, answering the clansman's questions. He explains that they are from the clan of Geats, and that his father's name is Extheow. They heard of the terror that has been wrecked on Hrothgar and have come to help slay the monster once and for all.

After hearing their story, the clansmen happily grants the warriors passage across the land. He promises to send men to guard their boat while they are trying to kill Grendel so that they can return home safely. The clansman shows them the way to Heorot, and eventually they come to the great hall, which is the most beautiful building in sight. The clansman leaves the warriors, wishing them luck before he returns to guard their ship.

V

When Beowulf and his men get to the great hall, they set down their weapons and armor to rest. A warrior of Hrothgar approaches them and asks who they are, remarking that he has never seen men with so much armor before. Beowulf greets the warrior, giving him name and asking to speak to Hrothgar himself. The warrior tells them to wait while he asks Hrothgar if he will see them.

The warrior goes to where Hrothgar sits, still surrounded by his men though he is now old and gray. He gives Hrothgar the news that there is a group of warriors who wish to talk to him, and advises Hrothgar to listen to them because their leader looks like a mighty hero.

VI

Hrothgar tells Wulfgar, his warrior, to welcome the group in. Hrothgar knew Beowulf's father, and has heard tales of Beowulf's legendary strength. He is glad that such brave men have come to help him in his time of need, and intends to welcome them as honored guests. Wulfgar travels back to the band of warriors with his message of welcome from Hrothgar. He says that they will be allowed inside Heorot in their armor, but insists that they leave their weapons outside. Beowulf and his warriors leave their weapons, and a few men stay behind to guard them.

Inside, Beowulf greets Hrothgar very formally. He goes into detail about some of his famed battles, and asks Hrothgar for permission to kill Grendel. Beowulf wishes to fight Grendel in single combat, and since Grendel does not use weapons Beowulf does not intend to either. He vows to either kill Grendel or be killed himself. Beowulf does have one request though, and that is in the event of his death that Hrothgar send his armor back to his land since his body will be eaten by the monster.

VII

Hrothgar responds to Beowulf's request by recalling the actions of his father, who killed Heatholaf of the Wylfings and sailed to Hrothgar who had become the ruler of the Danes not long before. Hrothgar settled the argument by sending a tribute to the Wylfings, and after that Ecgtheow swore his loyalty to Hrothgar.

Although Hrothgar does not wish to ask others for help in solving his problems, the situation with Grendel has become so desperate that he has no choice. He tells Beowulf that he may fight Grendel, but warns him that many other brave warriors have come to Heorot vowing that they would kill the famed monster. None of them succeeded and are now dead. Nevertheless, he invites Beowulf and his men to sit down and feast with them.

VIII

A man named Unferth spoke up during the feast. He was envious of Beowulf's achievements, and tries to undermine him. He asks Beowulf if he is the same man who swam across the ocean despite great risk to himself and lost to Brecaa. Even though they fought for seven days, Unferth mocks that no one has lasted one day against Grendel despite their bravery.

Beowulf calmly replies to Unferth with his own version of the story. He tells Unferth that he must have drank too much beer and not remembered right. Both boys, he and Breca decided to swim the ocean. They took weapons to defend themselves, and set out. They swam for five days before a huge storm overtook them. Sea monsters were awakened, and one of them dragged Beowulf down to the deeps before Beowulf managed to kill it with his sword. Monsters continued attacking, but Beowulf killed them.

IX

By the end of the night, the shores were safe and no sailors ever had trouble in those waters a gain. Beowulf came to shore unhurt but exhausted. He takes a break from his story to mock Unferth, saying that he has never fought a battle like that, and also pointing out that if he were as brave as he talked, Grendel wouldn't be going around terrorizing the Danes. Although many brave men have died trying to defeat Grendel, Beowulf is confident that he will be victorious.

After hearing this tale, Hrothgar and his hall became joyous. The Queen comes out with a cup and gives it to Hrothgar to drink. After he drinks, she takes the cup to everyone in the hall before stopping at Beowulf. As he takes the cup, Beowulf gives a short, formal speech, reiterating his confidence. The Queen sits down next to her husband and the feast continues.

When the sun sinks down below the horizon, Hrothgar and his men leave. Hrothgar remarks that Beowulf's group is the first he has ever left in the hall alone, and promises that if they defeat Grendel that they can ask for anything they want within his power.

X

Hrothgar and his men leave the hall for the night. Beowulf casts off his armor and sets aside his weapons. He gives a speech to his men, reminding them of why he is going to fight Grendel with armor, sword or shield. Beowulf then asks God to grant the victory to whoever is in the right. After his speech, Beowulf relaxes while his men lie awake in bed. None of them know for sure if they will go back home. In the dark, Grendel makes his way towards the great hall.

XI

Grendel makes his way to the great hall from the swamp. He sees the heroes, all asleep, and walks in with eyes aflame. He laughs when he sees them sleeping, and thinks about how he will kill them all before sunrise. He grabs the warrior closest to him and kills him, drinking his blood and eating his body piece by piece until there is nothing left. After his feast, Grendel moves towards the great hero who is reclining thinking to take him next.

Beowulf has been awake the whole time, and has watched Grendel devour the warrior. Grendel thinks about leaving, but suddenly his fingers are caught by some enormous strength. Beowulf has ahold of Grendel's hand, and for Grendel is afraid. He thinks of his safe den back in the swamp, and breaks free trying to escape. Beowulf chases after him, and the hall awakens.

Everything is chaos; the warriors are awake, and some of the Danes have come back. They see Beowulf fighting Grendel, and are amazed at the destruction that the two inflict on the hall. They are surprised that it is able to stand such an intense battle. Suddenly they hear a terrifying wail - Grendel is injured and Beowulf has him pinned.

XII

Beowulf and Grendel are still struggling in the hall, and the warriors around them try to help by striking at Grendel with their swords and spears. However, none of their weapons can pierce Grendel's skin because he is protected by a powerful spell. Despite this, Grendel begins to lose strength and gives in to Beowulf, whose grip on the demon is so strong that Grendel's very bones and muscles begin to give away. Finally, Beowulf succeeds in ripping the entire arm off Grendel, who knows he is going to die. Grendel is driven out of the hall and goes back to his lair in the swamp to die.

Beowulf has once again proven himself, and saved the Danes from the evil terror of Grendel. As proof of Beowulf's bravery, the shoulder and arm Beowulf ripped off of Grendel was mounted on the wall of the great hall.

XIII

In the morning people traveled from all around to the hall in order to see proof of Beowulf's victory and to celebrate. They looked at the footprints Grendel left as he fled the hall and followed them all the way to the demon's lair in the swamp. In Grendel's den they found large amounts of blood, and also realized Grendel had drowned himself in the muddy waters. Sure that his soul was now in hell, the clansmen rode home from the swamp in a joyous mood.

Tales began to spread of Beowulf's glory, and he was hailed as the most valiant warrior in the world. However, the Danes remained loyal to Hrothgar, their king. Songs began to be sung about Beowulf, and he was likened to the legendary warrior Sigemund. During his life, Sigemund was famous for killing monsters but his crowning glory was killing a vicious dragon that had a horde of treasure. Sigemund slew the dragon with his sword and took the gold back to his kingdom.

Eventually, Hrothgar himself came to the hall in order to see the proof of Grendel's destructions, and brought his queen with him.

XIV

Hrothgar reached the hall and saw Grendel's arm on the wall. He is very grateful that Grendel is dead, and admits that he had lost all hope of Grendel ever being killed. Beowulf, however, succeeded in vanquishing the evil terror, and for that Hrothgar offers Beowulf any wealth in the kingdom. He goes even further, announcing to all the warriors and clansmen that he will think of Beowulf as one of his own sons from that day forth. He says that Beowulf's fame will spread throughout the world, and that his name will never be forgotten.

Beowulf responds to Hrothgar, telling him that he is happy to have killed such a terrible monster. The only thing he wished is that Grendel had died in the hall instead of escaping back to the swamp. Beowulf says that everything happened as God had planned, and that there is still the proof of Grendel's arm to satisfy the king.

Throughout the speeches, Unferth, who had mocked Beowulf earlier and tried to undermine his strength, remained silent. The arm Beowulf took from Grendel was hard, and the claws described as being made of steel. It was obvious that a sword could never have severed the arm from the rest of Grendel's body, and so the fact that Beowulf ripped it off is proof of Beowulf's enormous strength.

XV

The men and women gathered in the hall began to clean and repair it for the upcoming feast to be held in celebration of Grendel's death. The hall, however, was in bad shape from the fight. Only the roof was untouched by the fierce battle waged the night before. Eventually, the hall was ready for the feast and Hrothgar himself arrived to attend the banquet. Noble men from all over the land traveled to Heorot in order to celebrate with Beowulf and Hrothgar, and they drank merrily.

During the feast, Hrothgar bestowed many gifts upon Beowulf in payment of his mighty deed. He gave the warrior a new set of armor, a battle banner woven with gold and a splendid sword. Beowulf drank in the hall with everyone else, and he was not ashamed to be seen receiving such valuable gifts in front of his men because he knew he deserved them.

Hrothgar had his men lead in eight war horses. One of the horses had a saddle that was set with jewels; Hrothgar had used the saddle during his battle days, and gave it graciously to Beowulf along with the other gifts.

XVI

The Geats were also paid back in gold for the warrior that Grendel killed, and everyone admitted that if Beowulf had not been there that all the warriors would most likely have been killed by Grendel as well. The narrator remarks that through God, men are blessed with insight.

After this last gift, minstrels begin singing. One of Hrothgar's singers begins the tale of Finn and his sons. Finn was the ruler of the Frisians and his wife was named Hildeburh. She was also the sister of Hnaef, the ruler of the Danes. During a battle between the two warring tribes, Hnaef was killed along with Hildeburh's son. At these losses, and also the large amount of casualties on both sides of the battlefield, Hildeburh began to grieve.

A truce was offered, and the two sides made a treaty promising to treat each other fairly. Hnaef, a great warrior, was burned on a pyre beside Hildeburh's son. Hildeburh grieved over them both as they burned until their bodies were completely consumed by the flames.

XVII

Because it was winter, the Danes were forced to stay with Finn and his people until spring came. Although they kept the truce, the leader of the Danes, named Hengest, still harbored bad feelings towards Finn. When it came time for them to leave, they slaughtered Finn and his kinsman, taking his treasures and his wife back with them to Denmark.

The song is finished, and the Queen enters the hall, sitting next to her husband. It is noted that although Unferth did try to shame Beowulf that he still has a good reputation among the men because of his courage. The Queen speaks to Hrothgar, telling him that she supports him naming Beowulf one of their sons. She believes that when Hrothgar dies and her sons ascend the throne that Beowulf will be a friend to them when they need help. She looks over at Beowulf, who is sitting on the benches in between her sons Hrothric and Hrothmund.

About BookCaps

We all need refreshers every now and then. Whether you are a student trying to cram for that big final, or someone just trying to understand a book more, BookCaps can help. We are a small, but growing company, and are adding titles every month.

Visit www.bookcaps.com to see more of our books, or contact us with any questions.

XVIII

The Queen gives Beowulf a cup and gifts of gold and jewels. The pieces of jewelry she gifted Beowulf with were worn by other great men in the past, mighty warriors. When the hall erupts in talk and excitement about the gifts, the Queen tells everyone that Beowulf has earned them with his deeds. She says that Beowulf's name will never be forgotten, and prays that he will be blessed. She also asks that he be a friend to her children if they ever need him.

After her speech, the Queen returns to Hrothgar's side. When the feast is over, Hrothgar and his men leave to go to sleep. No one knows that a new danger is outside, waiting. The clansmen sleep with their weapons and shields nearby because they are always ready to protect their leader.

XIX

All those in the hall went to sleep. They did not know it, but another monster was coming to the hall - Grendel's mother. She had been banished to the swamps after Cain killed Abel. Cain became the father of all monsters, including her son Grendel whom Beowulf killed with the help of God. Now Grendel's mother, grieving over her son's death, comes to Heorot to avenge him.

She bursts into the hall with great strength, but because she is a woman her strength is a little less than Grendel's. The warriors in the hall wake up and Grendel's mother decides to flee. Before she goes, she grabs her son's arm as well as one of Hrothgar's liegemen and takes them back with her to the swamp. Beowulf was not in the hall to stop her because he was sleeping somewhere else that night.

Seeing the destruction caused by monsters, Hrothgar is saddened and laments that his grief will never come to an end. In the morning Beowulf comes into the hall, unaware of the attack the night before. He asks Hrothgar if he slept peacefully throughout the night.

XX

Hrothgar is offended that Beowulf dares to ask such a mindless question. Seeing that Beowulf does not know the night's events, Hrothgar tells him of the female monster who came to avenge Grendel. The man she took in the night was Hrothgar's advisor and one of his close friends, Aeschere.

Across the land there were tales of two monsters, one male and one female. The male was Grendel, and the one who attacked the great hall Hrothgar believes to be the female in the stories. The two monsters live in an extremely dangerous part of the swamp. It is so inhospitable that it has never been fully explored. The tales say that by night the water is lit on fire, and that all who have entered into the deep water there have never come out.

Despite this peril, Hrothgar asks Beowulf if he will once again be brave and come to the rescue of the Danes. If Beowulf is willing to follow the demon into the swamp and kill her, Hrothgar promises to give Beowulf large amounts of ancient treasure and gold.

XXI

Beowulf tells Hrothgar that he will gladly avenge the death of Aeschere. He remarks that everyone must die, but Beowulf plans on winning as much glory as he can before that happens. Beowulf vows to Hrothgar that he will track down Grendel's mother in the swamp, saying confidently that she will not be able to hide from him even if she decides to flee.

Beowulf has horses saddled and mounts on his own steed, leading his men off towards the swamp. They follow Grendel's mother's foot prints across the plain and the moor until they come to some cliffs. The waters at the bottom of the cliffs are dyed red with blood, and the men go to investigate. When they get to the shore, they are dismayed to see Aeschere's head floating on the waves.

Sea monsters are in the water, drawn to the scent of blood. The warriors sound their horns and the monsters begin swimming away. One of them is shot by the warden of Geats with his bow, and it begins to die in the water. The other warriors go over and finish it off with their spears, dragging it ashore when it is dead.

Beowulf appears, ready for battle. His armor is shining and he has his gold helmet on to protect him. In his hand is an ancient weapon called Hrunting. The sword was lent to him by none other than Unferth, who gave it to Beowulf after drinking at the feast.

XXII

Beowulf speaks to Hrothgar, reminding him that, if he should die in battle, to take care of his men and send his gifts back to his homeland. He then bequeaths his own sword to Unferth, in exchange for using the legendary Hrunting. With this, Beowulf says that he will either kill Grendel's mother or die trying before plunging into the water.

He swims most of a day before coming in sight of the bottom of the ocean. Grendel's mother realizes that she is being followed, and reaches out at him with her claws. Beowulf's armor, however, protects him from her attacks. Many sea monsters tried to kill Beowulf while he chases after the female demon, but he fends them off.

Eventually, Beowulf spots a hall which he guesses is Grendel's mother's lair. He sees her and swings Hrunting directly at her. Even though the sword has never lost a battle, it is incapable of piercing her flesh. Realizing that the sword is useless, Beowulf flings it aside in order that he can fight with his bare hands. Beowulf seizes her by the shoulder and she falls to the ground. Quickly she fights back, and the two grapple until Beowulf, spent, falls down. Grendel's mother takes a short sword and drives it at Beowulf in order to take her revenge. His armor once again protects him, and Beowulf is spared.

XXIII

After Beowulf stood, he saw the ancient sword of Eotens which, according to legend, was the most powerful sword in the world. It was made by giants and regular men could not swing it because it was so heavy. Beowulf, however, lifts the sword and, in one sweep, cuts off Grendel's mother's head. She sinks to the floor, the blade bloodied. After the demon is killed, a light blazes out. Curious, Beowulf looks around him to see if he can find the cause. As Beowulf walks down the hall, he spots Grendel's corpse. Angry at all the men Grendel had killed, Beowulf cuts off his head.

Above the waters, Hrothgar and the group see that large amounts of blood are turning the water red. It has been nine hours since Beowulf went into the water, and Hrothgar and his men give up hope of him returning. Beowulf's warriors, both fearing and hoping, wait to see if Beowulf will emerge from the depths.

Back under the water, Beowulf's sword is melting after touching Grendel's blood. The blade dissolves, leaving the massive jeweled hilt. Beowulf heads back up, noticing that since the demon has been killed all the sea monsters have disappeared. There are many treasures in the deep, but he takes only Grendel's head and the sword hilt as proof of his conquest.

Once at the surface, his men greet him gladly and thank God for his safe return. Grendel's head is so heavy that four men have to carry it back to Hrothgar's hall. When they enter the hall with Beowulf and the severed head everyone is amazed.

XXIV

Beowulf speaks to Hrothgar, announcing that he succeeded in killing Grendel's mother, and almost died in the process. However, he was shielded by the Lord. The great sword Hrunting did not do Beowulf any good, but he found an even greater weapon hanging on the wall. Although the blade itself disintegrated, Beowulf shows the king the hilt he brought back from the depths. He goes on to assure Hrothgar that his kingdom is now safe from both the evil demons, and gave him the hilt as a gift.

Hrothgar examines the hilt and is amazed at how old it is. The sword hilt is passed down through the generations, becoming a treasured heirloom that reminds the people of the trials they have overcome. Hrothgar speaks to Beowulf, telling him that he is grateful once again for saving the kingdom, and reiterates his promise to treat Beowulf as family. He calls Beowulf a true hero, and tells everyone that his name will pass into legend. Not only does Hrothgar consider Beowulf strong, but recognizes that he has wisdom as well. Hrothgar tells the story of the former king Heremod, who was a violent and unwise king, and warns Beowulf against ever becoming too proud.

XXV

Hrothgar continues his speech, telling Beowulf that he should not forget his own mortality. He is strong now, but one day he will be old and no longer invulnerable. Hrothgar himself believed in his youth that nothing could keep him from defending his people; the coming of Grendel got rid of those illusions. Hrothgar thanks Beowulf for killing both Grendel and his mother, telling him that in the morning he will receive his treasure.

He invites Beowulf and his warriors to sit and feast in celebration. Beowulf is glad to be able to sit down, and the banquet begins. After the feast, Beowulf goes to bed and everyone in the hall sleeps peacefully.

In the morning Beowulf and his warriors are getting ready to go home. Beowulf gives Hrunting back to Unferth, and even though it failed him in battle Beowulf still praises the sword and thanks Unferth for lending it to him. After graciously giving Unferth back his sword, Beowulf makes his way to Hrothgar.

XXVI

Beowulf speaks to Hrothgar, telling him that they plan to go back to Hygelac. He tells the king that if he ever has any more need of him to just call and Beowulf will come to his aid with thousands of warriors. He also says that if Hrothgar's son Hrethric ever comes to Geats that he will be treated as a friend.

Hrothgar answers him, telling Beowulf that he is wise beyond his years. He hopes that Beowulf will be a good leader, and expresses a genuine fondness for the young hero. Hrothgar declares that their two kingdoms will have a mutual peace, and will not hesitate to help the other in a time of need as long as he is alive. After the speech, Hrothgar presents Beowulf with twelve treasures to take back with him.

They bid farewell for a final time, and Hrothgar hugs Beowulf. Hrothgar has a feeling that he and Beowulf will not see each other again, and Hrothgar truly loves him as a son. After their farewell, Beowulf goes towards the boat.

XXVII

Beowulf and his men get to the shore, and greet the warden who was guarding their boat for them. They load the treasure and horses onto the ship, and Beowulf gives a golden sword to the man for faithfully guarding their boat. After loading up the ship, Beowulf and his warriors leave Daneland and travel back to Geatland. A guard was stationed on the cliffs of their homeland to watch for their return, and he comes to the beach to greet them. They bring the ship ashore, and he anchors it so that it will not blow away.

Beowulf asks the men to carry the treasure back home to where Hygelac dwells. Hygelac lives in a mighty castle and has a young queen named Hygd. She is a good queen, and is not prideful like the ancient queen who had men killed just for looking at her face. The ancient queen was named Modthyrth, but legend told that she became less cruel after marrying the mighty warrior Offa.

XXVIII

Beowulf goes quickly to Hygelac's castle, and Hygelac is told of the hero's return. After hearing the good news, Hygelac orders the hall to be made ready for Beowulf and his men, and when they arrive he greets them warmly. He offers them seats at his table, and wants to know everything that happened on their journey. He reminds Beowulf that he did not want him to undertake such a risky venture, but is glad that he is home safe.

Beowulf responds to Hygelac, telling him that he did succeed in killing Grendel and by doing so avenging all those he killed. He tells Hygelac that when he arrived at Hrothgar's hall he and his men were treated very well by both Hrothgar and his queen. During his stay, Beowulf overheard that Hrothgar's daughter is supposed to marry a prince of Heathobard, one of the Dane's former enemies. In the past, many battles were waged over land and there were many casualties on both sides. Beowulf is afraid that the marriage will bring the two clans too close and, being reminded of the wrongs done to the other, will start the fighting anew.

Realizing that he has gotten off track, Beowulf turns the tale back to Grendel. He tells Hygelac of how they waited for the monster in the great hall, and how he killed only one warrior before trying to ensnare Beowulf and getting caught. Beowulf is a good storyteller, and makes sure to make everything sound intense. He tells Hygelac that after Grendel was killed Hrothgar rewarded him handsomely and they feasted. That night Grendel's mother came and Beowulf was asked to follow her into the swamp to kill her in her lair. Beowulf tells Hygelac that he succeeded once again, and that Hrothgar rewarded him with even more treasure.

XXIX

Beowulf offers his kinsman and prince all the treasures that he received from Hrothgar. He knows that he does not have many remaining kinsman, and wishes to please his uncle. He gives Hygelac the suit of armour and ancient sword that was used by Heorogar, as well as four of the armoured horses. To Hygelac's wife Beowulf gifted three horses and a beautiful necklace. Beowulf was strong as well as wise, to treat his family so well. Even though Beowulf was stronger than most men, he did not commit violence needlessly or get into drunken brawls.

In return for his gifts Hygelac gives Beowulf an ancient heirloom sword of their family and lays it in his lap. He also gives him a large portion of land and a huge manor. After a few years Hygelac is killed, and his son cannot protect the kingdom. Beowulf becomes king of the realm, and rules for fifty years. After fifty years, Beowulf is old but wise, and a new danger presents itself. A Dragon lives in a nearby mountain range, and one day someone steals a golden goblet from its horde of treasure. Because of this crime, the dragon's wrath will be unleashed on all the people of Geatland.

XXX

The man who stole the goblet did not do so on purpose. He was fleeing from his master and sought shelter in the cave where the dragon lived. He saw the treasure, and then the dragon. Terrified, he ran out of the cave carrying the goblet that was in his hand.

The treasure belonged to an ancient lord, who hid all his possessions deep in the earth. He was the last of his people, and the treasure was his one pleasure. His people were killed in battle, and the ancient lord wished that the treasure would never be touched by another man. Eventually he died and a dragon found his treasure. This particular dragon was cursed to take treasure from graves and it stayed in that cave for three hundred years.

When the thief went back to his master and told them of the great treasure hidden beneath the ground, they decided to plunder it. When the dragon awoke, it was very angry and followed the men who stole its treasure. The dragon began to burn the country side, and eventually its wrath would cause Beowulf's end.

XXXI

The dragon continued to burn the land and people of Geatland, and eventually it even burned the throne room of the Geats - Beowulf's home. Beowulf, now old, becomes saddened at this tragedy. He thinks that it is his fault the dragon is terrorizing his kingdom and becomes bitter. Realizing that something must be done, Beowulf plots vengeance. He commands the welders to make an enormous war shield out of iron so that it cannot burn against the dragon's flames.

Beowulf knew that his life would end along with the dragon's. He did not fear the dragon, because even after he earned fame by killing Grendel and his mother he continued to fight many monsters and earn even more glory. He triumphed in the battle his kinsman Hygelac was killed in, and swam while wearing thirty coats of armour. After Hygelac was slain, Hygd welcomes Beowulf back to the kingdom and Hygelac's son took over the realm. However, he died in another fight against the enemies of the Geats, and Beowulf became a good and noble king in his place.

XXXII

Beowulf's first act as king was to take vengeance on the Swedes who had killed Hygelac's son. During his rule, he proved that he could overcome many perilous situations - until the dragon came.

Ready for his final battle, Beowulf goes with eleven other lords to seek the dragon. He had heard about the goblet that was stolen and finds the man who took it. Reluctant, the man leads Beowulf and his men to the cave where the dragon dwells every day. Although Beowulf is gloomy at his impending doom, he gives a speech to his men. He recounts his childhood, and how king Hrethel raised him along with his other three sons, one of which was Hygelac. One of Hrethel's sons was killed on accident by another, and this grieved Hrethel greatly. However, he could not take vengeance for his son's death without hurting his other son.

XXXIII

The king Hrethel's grief at losing his son was almost more than he could bear. He left his sons land and wealth when he passed away, and after his death there was a time of struggle between Sweden and Geatland. Beowulf fought in the front lines of the battle, and he preferred it that way. He ends his speech to the men by coming back to the dragon, declaring that he will engage in one more battle if the dragon will meet him outside the lair on open ground. He calls his warriors near and bids them farewell, explaining that he would rather not fight with sword and shield but that because the dragon is so powerful he needs a weapon to make the fight an equal match. He tells the men to wait farther away because the fight is his alone.

At the end of the speech everyone stands and goes to their respective places. Beowulf finds an arch of stone that has access to the cavern within. He cannot go down without risking being burned alive, and so he makes a war cry loud enough that the dragon can't help but hear it. The smoke and poison of the dragon's breath begins to come out of the cave, and Beowulf raises his shield and sword in preparation for the fight. When the dragon emerges, he and Beowulf regard each other warily. They are each afraid of the other, but the fight begins.

Beowulf's great shield does not protect him from the dragon's fire for as long as he would have wanted, and Beowulf lifts his arm and swings the sword, which does not pierce the dragon's flesh. Even though it was the best sword and shield in the land, Beowulf's protection failed him. Fire engulfs Beowulf, and his fellow comrades flee towards the woods. Only one remains, a noble kinsman of Beowulf.

XXXIV

The one warrior who remained behind was named Wiglaf, son of Weohstan. As he watched Beowulf struggle against the dragon's flames, he remembered all the good the Beowulf had done for him over the years. He drew his old sword, an heirloom from Eanmund, and faced the dragon. He called out to the other warriors, reminding them of their promise to Beowulf made before the battle. In the hall, Beowulf chose them because they were strong warriors and, although he wanted to slay the dragon for himself, he needs them to help. Wiglaf finishes his heroic speech by saying that he would rather die trying to help Beowulf than return with their noble king slaughtered.

With this, Wiglaf goes through the dragon's flames to help Beowulf. He calls out to Beowulf, giving him courage and reminding him of the glory and strength of his youth. The dragon's flames burn almost all of Wiglaf's armour away, but he manages to get behind the great iron shield with Beowulf. After hearing Wiglaf's bold speech, Beowulf once again has hope that he can defeat the dragon and save his kingdom. He strikes his sword at the dragon with all his strength and the sword shatters. The dragon strikes at Beowulf and gets him in the neck, and blood begins to spurt out of the wound.

XXXV

Seeing Beowulf hurt, Wiglaf reaches out even though his hand is badly burned and stabs the beast until its fire is lessened. Finally Beowulf is able to draw a knife and stab the dragon in another spot. Between the two of them, the dragon breathes its last breathe.

Slaying the dragon is Beowulf's last great feat, as he knows that the dragon's poison flowing through his blood will kill him. Beowulf walks to the edge of the arch and speaks to Wiglaf. He wants his kinsman to go down into the cavern and look at all the jewels and treasure. Beowulf reminisces about the fifty years that he was king of the Geats, and wishes that he had been blessed with a male hair to pass down his weapons and armour to. Despite the lack of an heir, Beowulf ruled with fairness and bravery. Beowulf wants to behold the treasure left behind by the dragon before he dies.

XXXVI

Wiglaf goes swiftly into the cavern to do as Beowulf wished. He sees mountains of gold and jewels, and treasures spanning many eras. He finds a banner woven with gold and picks it up. It gleams so bright that he is able to see everything. He grabs an armful of treasure and runs back up to the archway.

When he gets back to Beowulf, the elderly hero is greatly weakened by the lack of blood. Wiglaf, hoping to revive him, splashes Beowulf with water. Beowulf opens his eyes and sees the sample of treasure that Wiglaf has brought with him from the dragon's lair. He is thankful that he could live to see such treasure, and is grateful that he can leave such a gift for his people. He says he has paid for the treasure with his life, and tells Wiglaf that when he dies he wants to be buried on the headland. His burial will be called Beowulf's Barrow in honor of his memory.

Before Beowulf dies, he takes off his gold jewellery and armour, giving it to the brave young Wiglaf. He says his words of farewell, and his soul leaves his body to join his ancestors.

XXXVII

Wiglaf watches Beowulf as he dies, although it is very hard for him to do. He is sad that the hero is dead, but is thankful that the dragon who killed him is slain as well. With this last victory, he is able to say that Beowulf killed all of his enemies in battle. Beowulf paid for the treasure in the caverns with his death.

The other warriors who had hidden in the trees come out once they see that the dragon is dead. It is obvious from their walk that they're ashamed at their actions. They see Wiglaf splashing Beowulf with water, trying to wake him again to no avail. Death comes for every man, and Beowulf was not an exception.

Finally Wiglaf realizes that Beowulf is dead for good, and turns to the other warriors. Angrily, he accuses them of being cowards and not helping their king when they were needed. He says that the treasures Beowulf gave to them were wasted. He alone was able to help Beowulf, although he only succeeded in weakening the dragon by stabbing it long enough to allow Beowulf to land the killing blow. Wiglaf tells the men that the kingdom will know of their cowardice, and that they will not get any of the treasure left behind by the dragon. He says that it is better for a warrior to be dead than to live a life of shame.

XXXVIII

Wiglaf has the others announce the death of Beowulf to those who are anxiously waiting for news of the battle. The messenger goes around, telling the people that Beowulf's dead body lays beside the dragon that he slew and that Wiglaf is by his side, grieving. With their leader dead, the Geats believe that war is imminent, because historically after a great leader dies there is an upheaval with the surrounding countries trying to take advantage of the weakened state.

The messenger reminds the people of the story of Hygelac's fall. The messenger also says that he is sure the Swedes will attack them because of their long history of violence against one another. In times past, the Geats kidnaped Ongentheow's wife and the ruler of Sweden retaliated with war. Both sides fought at Ravenswood, and when hope seemed lost Hygelac came to rescue the Geats.

XXXIX

The battle between the Swedes and the Geats turned with Hygelac's arrival, and the leader of the Swedes, Ongentheow, realized that he was overpowered. Hygelac was a mighty warrior, and went after Ongentheow with his sword. A man named Wulf eventually smashed Ongentheow's head with his weapon, killing him. Ongentheow's brother took his sword and armour before fleeing back to Sweden. As a reward for killing the leader of the Swedes, Wulf was given riches, lands, and Hygelac's daughter in marriage.

The messenger finishes his story with a prediction that since Beowulf is dead the Swedes will want revenge for the death of Ongentheow. During Beowulf's reign they dared not attack, but Beowulf is no longer able to protect the Geats from the old blood feuds. The messenger urges everyone to go to where Beowulf's body lays next to the dragon, and get ready for his funeral. He also says that they should burn all the treasure that Beowulf won by fighting the dragon along with him.

At hearing these messages, the warriors become sad. They go to the cliff and find Beowulf's body stretched out beside the dragon. The great monster was enormous, at least fifty feet long where it lay dead. When they try to go into the cavern, however, they discover that the great mound of treasure cannot be touched by any human unless God allows it.

XL

The treasure in the cavern was placed under a spell so that no one who was greedy could touch it or enter the inner lair. Beowulf, however, had not wanted the treasure for himself but for his people. Wiglaf speaks, saying that the treasure belongs to the Geats, but that because of the sad way in which it was won it will be impossible to enjoy. He tells the people present how he fetched a sample of the treasure from below for Beowulf to see while he was still alive, and relates that he wanted to be buried in a burrow.

Wiglaf takes warriors down into the cavern to look at the great collection of treasure while others are busy collecting wood to make a pyre for Beowulf's body. He chooses seven men to go with him to the caverns, and they light their way with a torch. The treasure lying on the ground is easily picked up and there is so much of it that the men don't have to fight over what they want. Once out of the cavern, they push the dragon's body into the water and it is swallowed by the waves. After this is done, Beowulf is taken to Hrones-Ness to be buried.

XLI

The people of Geats make a huge funeral pyre and covered it with all sorts of armour and weapons, just as Beowulf wanted. They hold the funeral on top of a hill, and watch as Beowulf and his weapons burn. An old woman, grieving, dreads the days to come saying that they will be full of death and battle.

On the place where Beowulf's body burned, the people make a great mound. It takes them ten days, and they make sure that it is filled with all sorts of treasure. All this was done to mourn the passing of the greatest hero and beloved king that Geatland had ever known.

Made in the USA
Lexington, KY
21 June 2017